Beyond Broken Walls

Restore Our Hearts

"Those who do not control themselves are like a city
whose walls are broken down."
~Proverbs 25:28 NCV

Beyond Broken Walls

Restore Our Hearts

CALVARY CHAPEL OF DALLAS/PLANO
Women's Ministry*

2nd Edition 2020**+

**This 2020 edition entitled, "*Beyond Broken Walls, Restore Our Hearts*" was published by Syndeo Ministries with the permission of Calvary Chapel of Dallas/Plano Women's Ministry.

+Edited, reformatted, and revised by Debra K. Brinker. Content Consultation with Hannah R. Overton.

*The 1st editions were completed in a three part series which were entitled, "Confronting Giants-Part I" in 2012, "Confronting Your Giants-Part II" in 2013, and "Confronting More Giants-Part III" in 2014.

Syndeo Ministries
P.O. Box 3191
Palestine, TX 75802

ISBN: 9798632401111

Introduction

There is no shortage of brokenness around us. Tragedy, trauma, and disease are everywhere and are broadcast on every news station. Our lives are filled with broken places, and we carry the brokenness wherever we go. Damaged relationships, shattered emotions, deep sorrows, and other trauma not only make our hearts ache but can change the ways we act, react, and respond. These things can create broken places within us. We all know the feeling of being trapped in something that is broken.

But brokenness isn't an end in itself. Every one of our lives contains brokenness, but brokenness doesn't need to define our lives. Our broken places can leave a crack so the light can shine in!

No matter how broken we are, Jesus Christ can take us beyond our broken walls, and restore our hearts. In the midst of tragedy, heartache, pain, hopelessness, or sin; God is still faithful, and can rebuild and move us beyond our broken walls.

You are so worth it in God's eyes.

~The Syndeo Ministries Team

Syndeo Ministries
P.O. Box 3191
Palestine, TX 75802

Beyond Broken Walls
Restore Our Hearts

TABLE OF CONTENTS

The Battleground of the Mind

"…casting down arguments and every high thing that exalts itself against the knowledge of God, bringing every thought into captivity to the obedience of Christ."
~II Corinthians 10:5

1. How does the enemy make a battleground of your mind?

2. Consider how the enemy tries to find victory in your thoughts. How does he work? When does he work?

3. The Bible tells us to bring every thought into captivity to the obedience of Christ. What guidelines does the Bible give for what we are to think about? See Philippians 4:8

4. In combatting the enemy's lies and the sins and attitudes that ensnare us, what have you found effective in your own life?

5. What does II Corinthians 10:3-6 tell us about taking every thought captive in our lives?

6. What are we promised in I Corinthians 10: 12,13 regarding the temptations we face?

7. How does God encourage us in Isaiah 41:10 as we follow Him?

NOTES

"You and I are not what we eat; we are what we think." ~Walter Anderson

Section One

Fear
Discouragement
Anger
Bitterness
Lying
Deceit
Gossip
Guilt
Impatience
Procrastination

Fear

"...that through His death He might destroy him who had the power of death, that is the devil, and release those who through fear of death were all their lifetime subject to bondage." ~Hebrews 2:14-15

1. Define fear. What are some antonyms of fear (opposite words)?

2. What are some common fears? What do you tend to fear?

3. What do you know about God that would help you not be afraid?

4. Why does God say that we do not have to be afraid in these verses?

Deuteronomy 20:3-4

Joshua 1:9

II Chronicles 20:15

Isaiah 41:10

5. What have you found successful in fighting fear in your life?

NOTES

"Courage is fear that has said its prayers."
~Unknown

Discouragement

"Hope deferred makes the heart sick. But when the desire comes, it is a tree of life."~Proverbs 13:12

1. Define discouragement.

2. Under what conditions are you most likely to get discouraged? What situations cause discouragement?

3. Do you ever feel like giving up, like it's just too hard, like you can't do it? You are not alone. The Bible uses words like "faint," "disheartened," and "weary" to indicate discouragement. What is God's promise in Isaiah 40:28-31?

4. Psalm 77 is a Psalm of discouragement. But the writer didn't wallow in his discouragement. Review the Psalm. Why was he discouraged? How did he handle his discouragement?

5. Paul mentions in two places in the New Testament (Galatians 6:9 and II Thessalonians 3:3) that we can become "weary in well doing." How can we get discouraged while doing good works?

NOTES

"We find ourselves feeling low because we've lost per-
spective about Whom we're serving, why we're doing it,
and how God plans to reward us."
~David Jeremiah

Jealousy

"...For where there are envy, strife and divisions among you, are you not carnal and behaving like mere men?"
~I Corinthians 3:3

1. Define jealousy.

2. Jealousy is closely associated with covetousness in the Bible. What is the commandment concerning covetousness? Read Exodus 20:17. What does that mean to you?

3. II Corinthians 10:12 says that "those who compare themselves among themselves are not wise." What are some of the things we might be jealous of if we compare ourselves to others?

4. Jealousy begins at home. We see that in the stories of Cain and Abel, Jacob and Esau, Joseph and his brothers, and the older brother of the prodigal son, among others. Do you see the giant of jealousy rearing its ugly head in your family relationships?

5. What are the antidotes to jealousy?

Romans 12:15

Philippians 4:11

NOTES

"Envy is the art of counting the other fellow's blessings
instead of your own."
~Harold Coffin

Anger

"For the wrath of man does not produce the righteousness of God."~James 1:20

1. How would you define anger?

2. What are some synonyms of anger?

3. What makes you angry?

4. Psalm 37:4 tells us to cease from anger and forsake wrath, because it only causes harm. What harm have you seen anger cause?

5. The Bible tells us that there is a righteous anger ("be angry and sin not"). What do you think is the difference between a righteous anger, and an unrighteous anger?

6. What did God say to Cain regarding his anger? Read Genesis 4:6-7

7. Paul counsels us in Ephesians 4:31 to let anger in all of its forms be "put away from you." What does Ephesians 4:32 tell us to replace it with, and why?

NOTES

"Anger is one letter short of danger."
~Eleanor Roosevelt

Bitterness

"...I had great bitterness; but You have lovingly delivered my soul from the pit of corruption. For you have cast all my sins behind Your back." ~Isaiah 38:17

1. Define bitterness.

2. If bitterness begins as a root in our lives, what do we do (or not do) that allows it to grow and bear fruit?

3. In Matthew 18:21-35, we see a man who refused to forgive a friend. Because of his refusal to forgive, this bitter man was "handed over to the torturers." By allowing a root of bitterness to grow, we subject ourselves to inner torment. Describe the torment of bitterness.

4. Why and how can we forgive? See Ephesians 4:22

NOTES

> "Bitterness is like taking poison and waiting
> for the other person to die." ~Unknown

Lying and Deceit

"Do not lie to one another, since you have put off the old man with his deeds." ~Colossians 3:9

1. What is a lie?

2. Lies take many forms. What are some other forms of lying?

3. Define deceit.

4. The very essence of God's nature is truth. The Scripture says that He is truth and He cannot lie. His ways are true and He leads us into all truth. So, who is the father of all lies? (John 8:44)

5. How did Satan use deceit in Genesis 3:1?

6. Truth-telling is a matter of submission to God's will. What is God's command in Ephesians 4:25 and Colossians 3:9?

NOTES

Am I identifying myself with Jesus who is the source of truth or am I identifying with the enemy of my soul who is the father of lies?

Gossip

"A talebearer reveals secrets, but he who is of a faithful spirit conceals a matter." ~Proverbs 11:13

1. Define gossip.

2. What is the difference between libel and slander?

3. How do we find ourselves in situations of gossip without realizing or intending to?

4. I Timothy 5:13 tells about the "busybody." What does it say she does?

5. Write the prayer from Psalm 19:14 in your own words.

NOTES

"Gossip needn't be false to be evil - there's a lot of truth that shouldn't be passed around."
~Frank A. Clark

Guilt

"There is therefore now no condemnation to those who are in Christ Jesus," who do not walk according to the flesh, but according to the Spirit." ~Romans 8:1

1. Define guilt.

2. Is guilt the price we have to pay for our sins and failures?

3. When Jesus set us free, did He just set us free from the punishment of sin, or did He also set us free from the guilty feelings that follow our sin? What do you think?

4. Read Roman 3:23-26. What truth in verses 24-26 can give you peace and freedom from guilt?

5. What is the psalmist's cry in Psalm 130:3? In Psalm 130:4, how does he answer his question?

6. I John 1:9 is the antidote to sin and the solution to guilt. Write it below. When the solution is so easy, what lie does the devil tell you to keep you feeling guilty over a sin you have already confessed?

NOTES

35

"Guilt is the giant that is "the most invisible, but the
heaviest one of all." People are slowly suffocated
by the giant of guilt.
~David Jeremiah

Impatience

"...walk worthy of the calling with which you were called, with all lowliness and gentleness, with long-suffering, bearing with one another in love,..." ~Ephesians 4:1b-2

1. Define impatience. You may gain more understanding by looking at the definition of patience and long-suffering.

2. In what situations do you most frequently deal with impatience? What is the root cause of your impatience?

3. Patience (long-suffering) is one of the fruits of the Spirit listed in Galatians 5:22-23, one of the qualities by which a Christian can be identified. How do you observe patience in another?

4. The Bible speaks of patience in several contexts. Where should we exhibit patience?

Psalm 37:7

Romans 2:7

Romans 12:12

Ephesians 4:1b-2

Revelation 14:12

NOTES

"Not a one of us finds a delay easy to accept."
~Chuck Swindoll

Procrastination

*"...Go away for now; when I have a convenient time
I will call for you." ~Acts 24:25b*

39

1. Define procrastination.

2. Procrastination is a thief. What does it steal from us?

3. In order to be successful, procrastination relies on our believing lies. Give some examples.

4. "The ultimate result of procrastination is defeat." Explain how procrastination, particularly in reference to obedience to God, can spell defeat.

5. Read Luke 9:59-62. What do you learn about procrastination?

6. Read Acts 24:24-25. What was the price of Felix's procrastination?

NOTES

"Procrastination is opportunity's assassin."
~Victor Kiam

42

Section Two

43

Doubts
Grief
Loneliness
Hypocrisy
Addiction
Worry
Lust

Doubts

"Lord I believe. Help my unbelief!"
~Mark 9:24b

1. Define doubt.

2. When are you most likely to experience doubt?

3. David often expressed his doubt. Read Psalm 77:3-9. What doubt does he express?

4. In the same Psalm, verse 10-15, what does David say he will be doing to confront his doubts?

5. In Isaiah 49:14, Jerusalem expresses doubt by saying "The Lord has forsaken me, and my Lord has forgotten me." What is the Lord's response in verse 15-16?

6. Matthew 14:22-33 recounts the story of Jesus walking on the water. Peter joined him, but because of doubt, he began to sink. As Jesus saves Peter, how does He reprove him for his doubt?

7. What had Peter forgotten?

8. Thomas is the Bible's most notorious doubter. In John 20:25, we see his honest desire to test the evidence personally, as he basically says, "I'll believe it when I see it."
How did Jesus respond to Thomas in verse 27?

NOTES

"Turn your doubts to questions; Turn your questions to prayers; Turn your prayers to God"
~Mark Littleton

Grief

"...He has sent Me to heal the brokenhearted..."
~ Isaiah 61:1

1. Define grief.

2. Grief is a natural emotional response to what?

3. What has caused grief in your life?

4. Naomi had good reason to experience grief. Who did she blame in Ruth 1:13b, 20-21?

5. Events leading to personal grief can cause us to question God. How do Mary and Martha express this in John 11:21 and 11:32?

6. In John 16:33, Jesus promised that we will have tribulation in this life. We will experience trials and loss. How can the resulting grief be used in our life?

a. II Corinthians 1:3-5

b. James 1:2-4

c. I Peter 1:6-7

7. What do we know about Jesus, our High Priest, that makes Him the perfect One to turn to in times of sorrow and grief? (See Psalms 147:3; Isaiah 53:3-5; and Hebrews 4:15-16.)

NOTES

"As women of God, we have authenticity because we ourselves have come through the valley of sorrow and tears, and our faith remains stronger than ever."
~Vickie Kraft

Loneliness

"And the Lord God said, "It is not good that man should be alone..." ~Genesis 2:18a

1. Define loneliness.

2. We can experience feeling alone (disconnected, left out, isolated) even though we have others around us. How have you experienced loneliness?

3. Godly people in the Bible experienced loneliness. Look at these examples:

a. David - Psalms 102:6-7; Psalms 142:4

b. Jesus - Matthew 27:46; John 7:5

c. Paul - II Timothy 4:9-11, 16

4. What are we promised when we experience loneliness?

a. Psalms 27:10

b. Hebrews 13:5

5. What do you learn about God's purposes for the body of Christ from I Corinthians 12:24-25 and I John 1:7?

NOTES

"Look for yourself and you will find loneliness and despair. But look for Christ and you will find Him and everything else."
~C.S. Lewis

Hypocrisy

"If we say that we have fellowship with Him, and walk in darkness, we lie, and do not the truth."~I John 1:6

1. How would you define hypocrisy?

2. How did Jesus define hypocrisy in Matthew 23:3 and 23:28?

3. In Matthew 23:27, Jesus describes hypocrites as "white-washed tombs." Explain that in your own words.

5. Basically, it could be said that the hypocrite is "living a lie" or "playing church." How does Isaiah 29:13 describe this?

6. We can be a hypocrite in just about any Christian activity. The Bible mentions several. What are they?

a. Matthew 6:1-2

b. Matthew 6:5

c. Matthew 23:14

d. Matthew 23:23

NOTES

55

"...our Lord reserved His strongest and longest sermon not for struggling sinners, discouraged disciples, or even prosperous people, but for hypocrites..."
~Charles R. Swindoll

Addiction

"... that we should no longer be slaves of sin."
~ Romans 6:6

1. Define addiction.

2. How would you describe the symptoms of addiction, or the characteristics of an addict?

3. What are some common addictions? Some activities may not be sin in and of themselves; what makes an activity an addiction and therefore sinful? (see I Corinthians 6:12)

4. What does Matthew 6:24 teach us about anything that we allow to have mastery over us? How will our walk with the Lord be affected?

5. What does God's Word say about overcoming addictions?

a. Luke 1:37

b. Romans 6:16-18

c. Romans 7:23-25

d. Philippians 4:13

6. Read I Corinthians 16:15. What is an addiction that is acceptable? (Note: "devoted" = "addicted")

NOTES

____

____

____

____

____

____

____

____

____

____

____

____

____

____

____

____

"For the good that I will to do, I do not do, but the evil I
will not to do, that I practice."
~Romans 7:19

Worry

"Sufficient for the day is its own trouble."
~Matthew 6:34b

1. Define "worry" or "anxiety."

2. Why is worry a useless activity?

3. How is worry related to fear?

4. Read Matthew 6:25-34 and answer the following:

a. What components of everyday life does Jesus target?

b. What reasons does Jesus give in this passage that we have no need to worry?

5. As believers, what is our alternative to worry? (Philippians 4:6-7and I Peter 5:7)

6. What do you know about God that helps you not to worry? Sum up why a true Christian has no need to worry.

NOTES

"Worry does not empty tomorrow of its sorrows; it empties today of its strength."
~Corrie Ten Boom

Lust

"But each one is tempted when he is drawn away by his own desires and enticed."~James 1:14

1. Define lust.

2. Sometimes we think of lust only in a sexual context. But we could consider lust "the craving of the flesh." What do you learn about the lust of the flesh in Galatians 5:16-17?

3. What are other objects of lust which can grab hold of us?

4. Samson was a judge in Israel who was taken down by the giant of lust. Being consumed by lust, what does the Bible say of Samson in Judges 16:20b?

63

5. Joseph faced his temptations in a different way. When Potiphar's wife persisted in her attempts to seduce him, what did Joseph do? (Genesis 39:12)

NOTES

Lust: "…Its alluring voice can infiltrate the most intelligent mind and cause its victim to believe its lies and respond to its appeal."
~Charles R. Swindoll

Section Three

Disregarding Prayer
Neglecting the Word
Materialism
Debt
Busyness
Laziness

Disregarding Prayer

"...men always ought to pray and not lose heart..."
~Luke 18:1b

1. One of the joys of our salvation is that we can have a relationship with God. Any relationship requires communication in order to grow deeper. How would you define communication?

2. Is that how you would define prayer?

3. Read Matthew 6:8. Because God is all-knowing, there are those who might suggest that we don't need to pray. How would you respond to that?

4. What is commanded in Philippians 4:6?

5. When we neglect prayer, what will be lacking in our life?

a. Psalms 138:3

b. Jeremiah 33:3

c. Hebrews 4:16

6. We may neglect prayer because of our own weakness and feelings of inadequacy. Why is this no excuse, according to Romans 8:26?

NOTES

"Prayer is not a burden but a privilege- an incredible privilege which is ours."
~D. James Kennedy

Neglecting Your Bible

"...Your Word was to me the joy and rejoicing of my heart..." ~Jeremiah 15:16b

1. Read the following verses and explain ways that God's Word benefits us.

a. Psalms 19:7

d. II Timothy 3:16-17

2. Read Ephesians 6:10-18. What part does the Word of God have in our struggles with the enemy?

3. Why is the Word of God essential to our walk of faith according to Romans 10:17?

4. Psalm 119 gives us many of the benefits of God's Word in our life. Look at verses 9, 28, 50, 97-99, 105 and 133, and note some of them.

5. What commands are given in Colossians 3:16a and II Timothy 2:15 regarding God's Word?

NOTES

"When people stop reading or studying the Word, it's because they're eating the junk food of the world.
~Jon Courson

Materialism

***"...one's life does not consist in the abundance of the
things he possesses.~ Luke 12:15***

1. The Scriptures describe materialism. What will be the
result of materialism in your life?

a. Ecclesiastes 2:10-11

b. Ecclesiastes 5:10-11

c. Mark 4:19

2. What warning does I Timothy 6:9-10 give to those desiring
material wealth?

3. How can riches deceive you according to Revelation
3:17?

4. Romans 12:2a has been paraphrased, "Don't let the world squeeze you into its mold." How does the world exert its influence on your values? According to Romans 12:2b, what is the antidote?

5. Read Matthew 6:19-21, Colossians 3:2 and I Timothy 6:6-8 for some solutions to materialism (the pursuit of more and more things). Which Scripture speaks to you?

6. Matthew 6:32-33 gives us the key to contentment. What is it?

NOTES

"...whatever trinkets, toys or hobbies you're looking to
for satisfaction will never fulfill you. They'll never bring
about that which you hope they will."
~Jon Courson

Debt

"Owe no one anything except to love one another..."
~Romans 13:8a

1. The Bible neither expressly forbids nor condones the borrowing of money. But it does give numerous guidelines to encourage wise stewardship. How are the wicked and righteous described in Psalm 37:21?

2. What activities can affect our financial health according to Proverbs 21:17 and Proverbs 23:19-21?

3. How does Proverbs 22:7 describe your relationship to those to whom you owe money?

a. Nehemiah 5:1-13 describes the situation the Israelites were in because of debt. According to verses 35, what were they facing?

b. II Kings 4:1-7 recounts the story of a widow who was in debt. What was she facing?

4. Debt can be a yoke of bondage. What does Galatians 5:1 say that God wants for us?

NOTES

"Do not save what is left after spending, but spend what
is left after saving."
~Warren Buffett

Busyness

"Martha, Martha, you are anxious and troubled about many things…"~Luke 10:41-42a

1. Read Haggai 1:5-9. What has been keeping the people busy?

a. What have they neglected?

b. What advice does the Lord give them in verse 7?

2. According to I Corinthians 10:31, what should all of our activities do?

3. Martha was busy serving the Lord in Luke 10:38-42. Why did Jesus gently reprimand her?

4. What are the negative effects of your busyness on you? On those around you? On your walk with the Lord?

5. Time is a God-given commodity. What advice does the Bible give us in Ephesians 5:15-16 regarding our time? What does this mean to you?

6. In our society, busyness can be a badge of honor. Do you see the sin of pride in your busyness?

NOTES

"The One who instructed us to 'be still and know that I am God' must hurt when He witnesses our frantic, compulsive, agitated motions."

~Chuck Swindoll

Laziness

"(She) does not eat the bread of idleness."
~Proverbs 31:27b

1. Define laziness.

2. When and where do you most often confront laziness in your own life?

3. Read Proverbs 24:30-34. What are some of the dangers of laziness?

4. What do you learn about the lazy life from these verses in Proverbs?

a. Proverbs 10:26

b. Proverbs 12:24,27

c. Proverbs 15:19

d. Proverbs 26:14-16

5. One who is lazy has many excuses. What are your excuses?

6. What are some excuses used in these verses?

a. Proverbs 20:4

b. Proverbs 26:13

7. According to Proverbs 13:4, laziness has severe spiritual consequences. What is the difference between the soul of a lazy man and the soul of the diligent? Explain.

NOTES

____

____

____

____

____

____

____

____

____

____

____

____

____

____

____

____

"Opportunity is missed by most people because it is dressed in overalls and looks like work."
~Thomas Edison

85

About the "Free to Grow" Series

The Bible Studies that make up the "Free to Grow" Series were originally written by Calvary Chapel of Dallas/Plano Women's Ministry, who have graciously allowed Syndeo Ministries to publish all of the books in this series, including this 4th book, "*Beyond Broken Walls, Restore Our Hearts*" as part of a Bible Study Ministry.

The first three books of the series include, "By Faith: A Study of Hebrews Chapter 11", "The Acts of the Apostles", and "The Holy Spirit", all of which are available on Amazon or through Syndeo Ministries.

We are so happy that you have chosen to study God's Word and participate in the "Free to Grow" Series. We pray that this Bible Study, "*Beyond Broken Walls, Restore Our Hearts*" will speak to your heart and change your life!

For those completing this study as part of our Bible Study Program, we ask that you please write a short paragraph describing how it impacted your life. Upon receipt of your summary, Syndeo Ministries will send you two certificates: one for parole and one for you to keep. Also, please include a request for the next study with your summary paragraph. You can also request to be a part of the entire series.

Thank you to those who are part of the Pen Pal Program who are doing this study along with your "Sister in White." We so appreciate all you do as you walk alongside in Christ.

May God deepen the faith of each and every one of you as you study His Word. We are very excited to hear how God moves in your lives through this study!

~ The Syndeo Ministries Team

NOTES

NOTES

NOTES

NOTES

NOTES

NOTES

92

93

94